Susan,

GRAVEL
GHOSTS

with so much gratitude,

MEGAN MERCHANT

Megan Merchant

GLASS LYRE PRESS

Cover art: Joseph Stepaniuk
Design & layout: Steven Asmussen
Copyediting: Linda E. Kim
Author photo: Max Stepaniuk

Glass Lyre Press, LLC
P.O. Box 2693
Glenview, IL 60026

www.GlassLyrePress.com

CONTENTS

I

II

III

GRAVEL GHOSTS:

a leafless flower that occurs in sandy washes and dark, rocky, and clay soils in the Eastern and Northern Mojave Desert. The name was given because the spreading shroud of white flowers connects at the nearly invisible stem.

—FALCON GUIDE TO THE MOJAVE

I

ASKING, LEAVING

I hear the Japanese maples
slowly growing, dancing close
and shallow with the moon
under courtyard windows,
open to the trains.

I face their sounds—the ticking
song of what's lost,
misplaced, as if mere melody
could unearth desire.

And then everything turns
to wine, tongue slowing, train passing,
maples winding their way back
into the afternoon I wore, you wore,
the afternoon we made love on.

All days leave without asking.

STANDING WATER

Once I saw a Buick stranded
in a puddle that looked
no deeper than my knees.
The woman, hysterical,
climbed from her window
to the roof, arms reaching

toward the sky for a rescue—
oblivious that the clouds
had started it all, although
who's to say how long
they had been holding a storm

inside tempered enough
to draw out a small stream,
thick enough to engulf a passing plane,
flocks of swallows, tendrils of smoke
and dust.

Her father should have taught her
the proper technique for passing
through bodies of water,
how to cross the glassy onyx, when
to touch the gas, shift the wheel,

plummet the same direction as a slant
of light through drawn blinds
in an early hour. To turn her body
whole in the direction of her eyes,
the way a stream flows under rocks,
despite gravity. How the body follows.

GRAVEL GHOSTS

What haunts in this landscape of blankets and windows
is the low growl the wind makes when it tempers against
the glass, calling open acres across the main road, where

yesterday a coyote wandered into the stucco stretch of homes,
and you knew then, the feeling crossing you in sleep, tapping
alongside each delicate inhale, was your history

stirring. Not even the summer monsoons, the drainage
that collects low in the valley, the tolerant sage in the dry-walled
canyon, could predict such a survival. History catching up to you,

watching patiently while you hide your bags behind the carport,
half buried in bottlebrush and thicket, while you take your time
sipping wine in your bathrobe, slow and democratic,

as if you had every chime in the world stilled to your request,
but you still cannot hush this calling—it's in your bones;
gravel ghosts pressing coarse grains into your skin

while you dream the settled names of towns—Menomonee
Falls, Chenequa, Heartland—a red barn door, bales of hay tightly
wrapped in string, the catch of a loose door hinge, the picture

of your father holding you and the trout you caught in the same lake
that buried his father, how tight the sleeves of your shirt were,
or weren't, the picture hasn't been around for years now;

there isn't a need. Only a word that rustles your sleep,
sends you wandering the streets, crossings and lamp-
posts identical in every direction until all things are the
same, except you, frightened, scurrying away from night.

UNDER THE BODHI TREE

Light or without, it's there.
Poised and coiled in the damp
cellar, underneath the red wood
pier, in the clock and stillness of
an hour, when you look
at my wrist and say *Baby,*
I'm late. It has already arrived.
In the water dish, after fingers
dip and bless a dying forehead,
in the mosaic of an early spring,
it has found shape. In the semi-dark,
when you're there but half in sleep and
wanting, when your arms are folded
into themselves, when the geraniums
bloom, the silver comes clean,
the mail falls through the slit, when
a pigeon flies its way into an open
office window and you feel all the stranger.
It's there. When glasses crash
against the wall, when the poems
come clean, when the poems come
quickly, too quickly, and you haven't
written for days. Like a black-winged
beetle, the cicada song after June,
the wooden chimes on a windless
desert day, this day. In emptiness,
light or without,
it's there.

Learning to Float

I spent one afternoon
in a cornfield
with a boy
who didn't want
to be seen with me,
so we pressed
our hands between
rough stalks,
kissed in passing,
the horizon glinting
with grain elevators
and dust.

My childhood lips
were the dry rush
of a train,
something
to roar past, flush
with shame,
and then

I learned
to float, on my back
first, let the water
fill my ears,
hold the curves
of my spine,
the way, later,
my husband
would trace his hands
over my hips
in sleep,
to match the warm
density of dream
to my skin.

I grew tall in water—
muck-bottom lakes,
astringent pools,
ceramic baths,
cement showers—
it toughened my skin,
it became another body
to press into,
to form around the shapes
I would learn to mimic
in the dark.

ODE TO LONELINESS

after "Catalogue of Ephemera," by Rebecca Lindenberg

You gave me the slate-gray light of morning.

You gave me Bukowski and Yeats.

You gave me winter, a mirror of shadows, stretched nights.

You gave me hair in a ponytail, ripped jeans, a name at the bar downtown.
You gave me rowdy men and a jukebox, a reason for pockets on my ass.

You gave me topography, foreign collarbones and thick-knuckled hands,
matted tobacco hair, the closing-time taste of beer and *good enough,*
truck-stop sandwiches, matchbox lips.

You gave me mornings after, fetal, shivering in a bathtub, scrubbing
invisible indentations. You gave me nubby towels and smell of bleach,
starched and faded bedspreads. You gave me wildness.

You gave me monsoons that shook the walls so violently,
I pressed the smallest bones of my chest against them,
a conversation of vibration and heat.

You gave me solitude and the smell of burnt toast,
notes to myself—the unfinished poems.

You gave me dimensions. Which shapes my body could fit into.
The smallness of my wrists. You gave me the close static between bodies.
You gave me nearness.

You gave me an apartment with bare floors, then a basement
with wrought-iron bars over the smallest frame.
You gave me the absence of light.

You gave me flea markets and coffeehouses,
the antique table with deep wounds.

You gave me a year of blank-slated mornings, bitter coffee,
my fingers tracing watermarks and indentations. Someone else's history.

MOTHS AS BIG AS HUMMINGBIRDS

I.

Today I awoke unafraid of library fines, tourists, double-parked cars,
two-ply toilet paper, wasting time, wasting water, wasting the word *love*
on a Tuesday. I awoke unafraid of beginning as if on purpose,

unafraid of the sun, the slip of hours in a day that might lose me, two inches of rain or no
rain at all, the score of a baseball game that could predict a Second Coming, what it meant
to see a crow and pigeon pressing beak to beak in the park. I was unafraid of being the
only witness when everything stopped and I was left standing still, remembering motion.

II.

Today an August storm swept Death Valley, killing two, washing out roads, covering
parts of the park with suffocating mud, then lessening, soaking the soil as a gentle guest,
unfamiliar and tireless, in a land accustomed to hardly seeing water at all.

The landscape opened, unafraid of being historic, of being measured by scales of beauty
and shifting terrain, surfacing minerals, spreads of gravel ghosts, notch-leaved phacelia,
desert stars, moths as big as hummingbirds scattering seeds in all directions, their paths
abandoned in a three o'clock wind. Even the rocks are blooming a sulfur yellow—
widespread, daring.

I Deserve the Madness of a Loud Ending

Mid-sleep, you sit up, utterly displaced,
trying to identify the naked body lying in your sheets.

I wake, waiting for recognition.
Instead, you run your hand through my hair
it's all right ...

My mother chose my name from the book
she was reading while pregnant—

Meggie, the scandalous heroine who seduces a priest,
loves fiercely the unattainable,

and suffers romantically for four pages of bodily lust
that sustains an entire epic.

The legend of the thorn bird that impales
its sleek breast upon the longest, sharpest thorn

while the world stills,
listens to its song.

Before deciding, she tried it out several times
at the top of her lungs—*Meggie*—

loving the sound of anger it carried
almost as much as the story defining it.

Somewhere between sleep and waking,
you do not recognize my face.

Even after holding on to you, eyes closed,
I can describe the exact shade of your eyes, hair, strangeness.

My name goes here.

MARRIAGE

If you press your index finger like a plug
into your belly button, you can feel a shrill
vibe under the base of your penis, and it

makes you think you have to pee. You're drunk
and thirty, telling another man waiting in line to use
the toilet that you haven't stopped learning little quirks

about your body. How you must have hated me when I
called attention to the round protrusion your belly
made when you stood a little hunched in your old underwear,

or when I pressed a cold spoon heavily against your erection
to make it go down. But that's the beauty of marriage;
learning the difference between old and new. I trust you

enough to fall asleep on the stretch of desert between
Baker and Barstow—you allow this little pleasure, even though
you're tired and the landscape of dusted rocks has started to blur.

URBAN DEVELOPMENT

Burn a forest to farm and drain a pond to fish

—Unknown

They're bulldozing the hillside left of our home,
and inside we build lovely inarticulate speeches
with our toes—I bet you a dollar I can stand
on the tips of mine and you say *that's why*
we fit together so well. I come close,
despite the small tremors the wrecking
makes as they cut delicate shapes
into the hard stucco of earth with shrill
machinery; every now and sometimes
then a flute of smoke rises from the tip
of the crane and you comment on how beautiful
the fumes of destruction are in winter, as if
there is a natural connection to be made.

Ivanpah Road

Desert tortoises come out after rain.
Park rangers avoid dirt roads until they
can map what has washed away. Couples
park cars along the north side of Kelso,
haphazard, almost abandoned, to seek out
the most unlikely carpets of blooms—

spreads of hyacinth spaced along dried lake beds,
depressions of earth and deep basins. From the tip
of a desert dune, you can see spaces of soil between
each violet cluster and the morning air drying long

linear leaves. Out here, the heat tricks the thirst
of imagination; westerly shadows of stirred dust
become wet ravines, pooled water,
that after such flooding seem close, possible.

My Mojave prefers strays, distance. At least
an hour's walk for wildflowers that refuse
to give themselves away too quickly.

Ritual Root

The night before I married him,
I took a red plastic bucket,
heavy with water, and a shovel
to abandoned miles of desert.
Found a Yucca in the dimming
light, dug heavy at its
roots until my hands blistered from
the gravity of elements—
dirt pounds, granules of rock.
I pulled a handful of wet
root from the broken earth,
ground veins until they turned
to lather, and washed the deadness
of my hair.

NOTHING, ARIZONA

Driving through Nothing,
I am scolded for asking
what desert we are in
along the stretch of Highway 93,
when it is really a town—
three shanties, a rusted gas
stop, piled funereal
metal and heap. Sounds,

all passing, bits of heavy
rock, honking horns, timely
disruptions in a mapped space,
where time owns only

itself; deeply spiked ravines,
flat basins, arms of Joshua trees,
gardens of creosote bush, ocotillo,
and cholla cacti, and a sign
that reads LAST STOP FOR SIXTY MILES.

A man could die
in this evaporated openness,
or live with nothing to do but
think, shoot giant saguaros to
pieces, count cars, and still call it
a life.

I wonder if the residents
eat their meals in company,
share secret earths, interrupt
each other's sentences to break
the rural flatness of always being
heard. If, in this absence, they
are close, like family.

TIN-CAN LOVE

Today the terrain is blowing crazy—
land moving its sidewinding
body of loose skin, riding easterly gusts,
shaking squat mobile homes
and their tinfoil windows.

Those who live this Mojave life
want loneliness, heart calendars
set to the bloom time of a five-
petaled flower, May to September,
and if late due to an undue cold,
the heart will wait, and would, even
if it had something else to do.

It's a tin can kind of love, living on wheels.
A property line of cracked earth—the dry
lake bed—a lifeline, a claim. Even desert
dwellers own something.

A collection of topographic recipes,
perhaps, on inherited note cards—
> *For Flax Leaves: Crush leaves*
> *in a fist, tear the sweet flesh*
> *of petals, as a cure for swelling any parts*
> *of a body—lips, hands, even thighs.*

Those wildly inflamed
take the membranous skin
in their mouths
and swallow.

AFTER

I.
After the monsoons,
the cicadas
repeat everything.
We shelter indoors,
hiding from the
spindles of
grainy wind
that pelt the windows
and shutter daylight
into a rind-colored
sieve

and all of the words
that tasted thick
during the rain
begin to bone
with the sluggish
retreat
of summer.

Love,
you are not the ache
but the air trapped
thin between
my joints,
and when we rub
against
each other,

you howl,
as the wind
slides its loose-dust
body
against brick and
bark,
upending
what has not
been bolted
into place.

II.
After the dry storms,
once you clear
away a shorn
umbrella,
oil-stained
rags, and tumbleweed,
you'll find an unbroken
snakeskin flagging
the upturned branch
of a creosote,

an omen of a lasting,
sheeted winter.
When it arrives,
we'll stir
flakes of skin-shed
and lavender
into our tea,
spoons echoing
the clamor
of chimes
tuning the wind.

Stories Live in the Body

Begin by writing down the name
of someone you can't be with,
as if then it disappears
from your mind's grasp
onto the page,
to become simply that—
an omission.

But it's what we can't name
that comes to haunt us,
the pulse of memory in cells
that taste of cheap Bordeaux
and fresh empanadas, green olives
with the hint of red

currant, cells filled with the dull
ache of skin from the stubble
of his chin as it pressed
into yours when you whispered *I am a poem,*
so he'd know how to take you,
and you'd know how to forget,
line by line,

the way he bit the thin skin of wrists
before mouth,
you taste like morning,
or was it the other way around—
we choose only the details of what
it means to remember—except

on nights when the temperature drops
those few degrees it takes to become
an old weathervane of secrets,
and all of the papers with all of the names
worth forgetting
reappear,

26

fluttering outside locked doors,
where you lay, quietly existing—wishing
someone had lit a match to the pile
of tongues, thighs, arms, breasts,
thick striations of bone—slowly
letting each story burn.

CONCEPTION

You beside me,
half in sleep
and wanting,
as if the difference
could be divided
by waking.
I feel you, hard.

I let you
find your way,
hands cupped
around my belly,
then breasts,
then belly.
You push into me,
rougher
than I'd like,

which excites you,
makes you grab
a fistful of hair,
press my nipples
down as if their
natural rising
were an insult.

You bite my chin,
my cheeks,
build a pulsing
pressure with
the weight
of your thighs—
muscle gripping
bone, gripping
muscle,

making a sheath
of skin, curls
thick with
black hair,
and I know
you're so far-gone
that a train
could plow down
a stalled car
on the tracks
outside our window

without you
so much as saying
oh shit
when the chunks
of twisted steel
grind into gravel,
skid over rusted
iron tracks,
the driver's head
bleeding onto the horn—

we're so graphic,
I want to pull over and look.

And when you finish,
you shift
your weight
from body to bed,
waiting for sleep
to soak back
into fingers, thighs,
lips, and dream.

I rush
to the bathroom,
squat down
on the toilet,
let the silky
stream slip
downward,
making the smallest
splash of wet
on wet,
and pray
this isn't the one
that will bring us a child.

CONSEQUENCES OF COLD

Because I'm sick, we celebrate our first six months with glasses of wine
on our living room couch, watching the Weather Channel report a record
cold across the Mojave. The weatherman keeps saying *protect your pets
and your pipes from freezing,* so you sneak outside with ragged towels,
a flashlight between your teeth, covering anything left exposed. I watch
the shape your body makes wandering around the acre plot in the dark
in search of plumbing, approximating the consequences of cold. And,
after a while, fall asleep listening to the settling sound of water freezing.
You carefully scoop my head under your arm and carry me all the way
to bed, whispering *you'll feel better soon.* The pond outside slowly
changing into something a little easier to contain.

II

ONE HUNDRED-YEAR BLOOM

*From my rotting body, flowers shall grow and I am in them
and that is eternity.*

—Edvard Munch

How many chances in this life
do you have to meet yourself
as someone else? To come
back to the land where you
were born, only to find,
among boarded windows,
cracked pipes, shorn shingles,
that you have already left,

trees mindless of the man
who once soiled their roots,
tended to a violet patchwork
of Cattleyas when the evening
frost called in an emergency
of night.

How instinctively you would
grasp the thinness of their leaves
in a cupped palm, draw them close
to your lips, whisper heat and breath
to keep them through wintry hours.

When, exactly,
did you stop listening?
How long has this landscape
of your past been receding,
without a phone, just a junction box,
frayed wires, a stranded motorist
in the desert calling out random numbers,

letting it ring and ring, waiting for
an answer, a voice to recognize
and say *Yes, Stranger, you are alive.*
But no one's home. No one.
The greater parts of yourself
are living someplace else.

In the morning when you wake,
you feel a loneliness of having kept
something alive long enough to let die
another night, with another choice.

DOOR COUNTY

I close everything into a glass bookshelf
to keep the shape, bindings that prove
nothing was ever taken from a book
of poetry, and instead of writing,
spend hours watching you pick
through the grass, head and back
bent in concentration.

We've only been in my childhood
home for three afternoons when you burst
between the wooden doors, hand
me a four-leaf clover you find behind
the garage, and pick it like my grandfather
used to do, insisting I press it
between pages. As if you know

the tradition. We retreat to the porch, where
the sun draws a dusted heat and the June
fishing boats reel into the dock
around five, dragging lines of bass,
walleye, and pike.

I listen to the calming noise
of their complaints, rivets of old
propeller engines and the clinking
dinnertime preparation—washing Mason
jars to use for wine that you'll drink
in my father's wicker chair, as if
nothing has aged, only been replaced.

Except when the humidity settles into night,
the doors and windows let in less air
through ducts that once hummed
dreams into sleep. And a glass night-light
shapes each picture lining the stairwell,
that, in spite of memory, pledges things actually
happened. Things before you that were picked
to disappear.

ONE

This paper is a tree
rooted in sun, clouds, ocean, and rain.

This paper is the man who cut down the tree,
his wife, their children, the cornmeal and tea
he ate last night, the electricity that feeds the night-
light in the quiet hallway of dawn when he wakes
and kisses each child sweetly, leaves with
the taste of dreams on his mouth.

This paper is something forgotten, something moved,
misplaced, buried thick in skin so adamantly not there
that it changes the ridgeline of flesh.

It is a lover you think of when you see men
quietly sitting, reading the paper over coffee,
something he never did in front of you, not even in dreams.

It is the town you grew up in, the private memories
of strangers you find scrawled on the backs of bathroom
stalls—*John loves Stella*—, so permanent that you believe,
in that moment, they are infinite.

Like the tinged-yellow fingernails of a smoker,
the height a swing can arc, the question when
he says *maybe you are the answer tonight.*

This paper is nothing more than the grain of sand that
loosened a whole generation, a splinter of kindling
stuck into a finger, the reassurance of blood
that follows, and the voice that whispers *show me what is real.*

This paper is an entire season of loss, the first bloom
of a Japanese Maple so visually loud that it stuns an entire street
into breaking every inch of glass—frames, mirrors, windows—
to make an echo from fragments of pain.

This paper is a pigeon balancing on a rooftop,
a child pressing her palms into freshly laid cement,
the symphony that finally stops trying to mimic
the soft whisper of planes.

It is emptiness left asking *empty of what?* which is the only way
to be full, loosely connected like a swift-moving acre of water.

Saint Rose's Recipe for Piety

How to create suffering
where
there is none:

When
they adorn
your head
with a wreath
of roses,

dig the pin
sharply
into your
skull,

puncture there.

When working
from scratch,

substitute
emptiness
with the throb
of incessant
prayer.

And, because
there's
no absolution

for the kind
of beauty
that could
unravel
the whole
world,

take
a scoop
of crushed
pepper,

rub
like sand
into your
cheeks,

grain
by coarse
and blistering
grain,

imagining
each scream
of self-inflicted
pain

is the sound
of ocean
waves

coming
closer
to the shore.

SCARRING

[orchids] derive their nutrients from the atmosphere, rain water, litter, and even their own dead tissue.

—Orchidaceae

Men in orange hard hats are laying a stink of blacktop
on the roadway, digging chunks of rough-edged mountains,
refining the earth to make room for modern, energy-efficient
houses that will sit on concrete embedded into the crust of rich
brown dirt. I am going blind in one eye. And wander the scarred
paths the bulldozers make before I lose my perspective, looking
for the tender rareness of orchids that grow in fissures between
rocks. I have nothing but pockets, hands, and tissue to wrap the
tangled clump of roots to carry home. And even though it's cold
and sunless, and I know the flowers will not take to the water
or soil, I select an old clay pot.

Pastoral

Sitting on the porch steps,
watching the tree tips mimic a full wave,
you tell me about the farmer down the road
who was trapped underneath a piece of machinery
and how the wind was blowing just right
so you could hear his calm screams
a mile away, while his wife, watching
Wheel of Fortune in their living room,
sat oblivious until the volunteer ambulance
arrived. It was a miracle he survived the crushing
weight trapping his pelvis and legs.

You attribute his survival to good nature;
not God or fate, but his sensibilities.
It's the only piece of news you have,
so we fall silent until the hoof and clatter
of a frenzied horse kicks up patches
of rain-heavy mud, spooked by a single car,
running fence-long, post to post, bucking
as the car's fender dips and raises in a rush
of speed, past the gravel, the gate, the two
of us sitting, saying little, except *I cannot believe
how fast they drive these lonely country roads.*

Ways to Worship

Every Sunday, our neighbor across the lake
shot off a Civil War cannon. The stink
of gunpowder would wallow past the tipsy
wooden fishing boat tied to our dock, through
the barn, across the spread of corn, soybeans,
right into our kitchen.

My mother and I would sit in the wheat-colored
light of morning, with coffee and crosswords,
waiting for the jarred discharge, the bloom
of sulfur that left an acerbic taste to our lips.

That was our signal to start the day—hauling water
in bright plastic buckets for the horses, baling hay,
mowing eight acres of grass, pulling weeds—
a routine preservation.

We'd work the whole day, waiting for the
mortar perfume to fade from our clothes, hands,
hair—so familiar, it smelled like the church I attended
as a child, the rows of candlelit prayers flickering
under a low ceiling, someone's plea burning in silence,
no matter how desperate the prayer.

The smoke of incense speckled over heads
of congregants on saintly days, holy celebrations,
and when touched by the blessed air, one by one

they traced the sign of the cross, thumb and forefinger,
onto their foreheads. *Amen.* Asked to pray for intentions
held in each beating heart. *Amen.*

I could never decide which was more reverent—
waiting for the boom and blast of an old war
machine that shot like clockwork, or asking
God to deliver a stranger's unknown prayer.

MIDNIGHT LIGHTNING

I have been through storms more remarkable
but was startled by the way you said
it's all right, go back to sleep
the night you climbed out of bed
to stand naked in front of the window.
There is a quiet privacy in desert lightning.

The night my grandfather lay dying in a hospice,
I climbed down to the docks and sat in thunder and rain
to feel the vibrations against my chest,
until my hysterical mother pulled me inside
to keep me from getting sick.

I have always felt that the remarkable intensity of crashing
meant that I was home.

Until I wake to you quietly climbing out of bed
and notice, more than your nudity,
how your whispering,
in a room full of lightning,
occupies the small bones
of my chest.

Filling Station God

Tabloids found in the checkout aisle bemoan
"God Found Eating Cheesecake at Mad Greek Café with Elvis,"
the all-night diner in the desert,
outside the city of sin without walls, just dust
that rides you across the California border

like fiberglass shards itching your hands,
squeezed along the 15 by big rigs
with decals —*Jes   ves   u*— peeling
and half mud-splattered Greek.
Above heat, the gas gauge siphons down to E.

Instead of praying, you pull out a map,
logistically chart the miles,
then, in silence, think back to your God;
how, at twelve, you feared the signs of a statue,
three stories high in an alcove, the town gathered

to see the miracle, see the stone hands bleed.
DNA tests proved human blood,
a task too elaborate for any local high schooler.
They shipped clergy from the Vatican to investigate faith.
Found you the fraud; bleeding marble, two car accidents

you shouldn't have walked out of, a flood;
death and disease didn't turn your head upward.
Only now, driving on empty in silence,
do you contemplate being filled.

ALCHEMY

Your friend invents
a burning log made
of natural elements
that doesn't leave
a black ash
or chemical toxin
from flame.
It burns invisible,
adding traceless
water vapor
to the air,
making night a little
heavier to inhale.

It's perfect for a campfire
in the dry rock desert,
where dark temperatures
dive from
daylight hours in a rush
of land and light, leaves
and salt, floodless channels
filled with a layover
of bony heat
and displaced spines
of tumbleweed
that spill shadows
on ravine walls.

Each shape
keeps company
until the log burns
itself to exhaustion
and you're left
alone, dim, cold,
the evidence
soaked deeply into skin.

III

Dry Storms

We're cursed with stray lightning strikes,
random flashes that ignited a block of homes
adjacent to a stretch of dry, rotted land.

Three were vacant, bank-owned, with weedy lawns,
a litter of dead pigeons in the driveway, no one home
to rush out handfuls of memories, no one home to die.

I always thought I'd know the instant
I'd be sharing my body—a small flutter,
the lilt of a heart in my belly.

I worry instead, by the window at night,
because I can't feel a damn thing, looking at lampposts,
night-shaped trees, a flicker of lightning without rain.

HE SAID

he was looking for something to make him complete.
I told him about the guitar that sits in my room un-played,
because I never learned the chords or how to read notes;
too busy with the close necessities of life—how, every week,
I dust the sleek body and strings so it looks ready
to play a sound, rather than quiet regret,

and how, on Tuesday, a dove trapped his plump-
winged body in the stucco alcove above my window,
spending the whole day there, as if by choice,
and I, too, listening to the tenor of his deep-belly
coo, wondering how he would find his way out,
and what was so worth diving that beautiful
bird-fat into such a small space—

as if his modest brain could even comprehend
such dimensions as to what shapes fit us
completely—or, maybe he knew he was dying
and wanted nothing more than to hear
the horribly choreographed music
the living make.

SMALL BIRTH

When you leave a room, is there an echo
of light where your body was, a sulfur or flint
that, when pressed against granite, sparks?
Were you light, my baby, or rock?

We had one conversation in a dream, in an unborn language.
It was fall. You pointed to the changing maple trees
on the roadside, little painter, and accused God
of getting it all wrong. *It wasn't supposed to be that beautiful.*
Nothing that stays with you ever is.

I asked the doctor how the unborn are able to breathe,
tucked in a body. How much landscape they remember,
what elements they already understand. *The same*
sorrows about life that you do, he said.

Small sculptor, size of the thin scar
on my right arm. At three weeks,
you came from soil. Wide empty spaces,
with a cold history waiting for your un-birth.
Sweet child, sleep next to my granite heart.

Traction

The doctor calls us back
the next day for a scan,
slides a wand
with a condom slipped over the head
between my legs.
It sees without sentiment,
the way I want to respond
when she says
I expected to see more growth.

We lose the baby on a Tuesday,
find out about its twin
on Thursday,
after they've already
removed the first with a vacuum.
Everyone says
God has a greater plan.
It's not for us to understand.
But there are words for it—
blighted ovum, tilted uterus—
that even a dictionary can explain.
Understanding is not the same as accepting.

My husband drives us to the hospital
for a second surgery,
a second loss.
They give me a pair of beige socks
with traction stickers along the bottom,
as if I'll be able to leave
the sterile bed,
stand on my own
long enough to slip.
As if the ground is level
for everyone but me.

PRAYER TO OUR LADY OF EXPECTATION

Bless this body
as fissure,
radiant
as fish scales
shimmering
in a backyard pool
under a yellowish
moon.

Bless the faithful
that congregate
there,

the way thunder
rattles the scummed
pile of bone-colored
dishes, glass
unsettling
glass.

Forgive
the seekers
of beauty and green lights
who rush oncoming
cars, those who loosen
their clothes
for virtue.

Bless the occasional
women,
the ephemeral
and crazed women,
those straddling
the median,
vibrating
like a windsock
of pain.

54

Bless the baptismal
storm
that unhinges
the door
from its frame

and the fractures
of lightning
that distort,

the flippant
wave of hand
that invites
the rain,

but, most of all,
bless the fetid
soil that refuses
to absorb
even
the smallest
drop.

Molecules

Because it's inelegant table talk,
I dream of them—my dead
babies—as cardboard cutouts,
walking single file
in mountain-shadowed
snow. The nameless
are impossible to call
home.

Mouth wide as sorrow,
I sleep hungrily, gulping
particles of air that, in dream,
we share.

I read once that
air is the inextricable
thread that twines
all the way to Jesus
and Buddha,
that we may be inhaling
skin cells and spit
from every person
who has participated
in this exchange of living.

I call out to my babies,
floating, untethered to any history.
Elegant. Almost
unwritten.

Sappho

I am accustomed
to throwing lit matches
into water
just to hear
the quick sizzle,

sound and sight
extinguished
in one line—

it's not you,

an inexactness in body,
composed of 80% water,
20% words,

that hold
until summer,

when splinters of dust
come in hot winds

and pavement compels feet bottoms
to water,

where I float, palms down,
Cristo Redentor,
stone arms in waiting.

Only Sappho really knew
the beauty of not being
able to throw her arms
around the world.

Even after the clergy
burned her short
lines,
I can hear her
Greek floating—
these inadequacies
ignite us.

March Miracle

We leave empty
metal buckets
on the porch,
shuffle
containers of rain—
starved plants
from under the awning
brightly into night
to publicize
the story of an otherwise
dead season,
hopeful.

We are equal
parts damaged
and luminous.

Silhouettes
glowing sharp as scars,
pleading
for a late-season rain.

I put on a pot
of coffee, you ready
a fire and blankets,
prepared to wait
out the night,
if necessary.

Our bodies,
our forgiveness
suspended,
so close to touching
that my arms
can feel the thin
static of air
grow heavier.

SOMEPLACE ELSE

Let's meet in the middle
of nowhere,
at a bar
with a single-syllable
name and sawdust
floors.

I'll wear
a hint of persimmon
and public transportation;
you'll press
your skin into old
books, pack
a bag full
of dead leaves,
and when
you see my eyes,
you'll want to take
off your shoes.

The TV behind the bar
will be on,
soundless,
and all of the letters

we've written
will pulse
when I place my lips
against the thin
skin of your
wrist.

We'll kiss and spit,
let the moments
dissolve
into the barroom
floor, easy to sweep
away.
You'll touch
each scar.
I'll memorize your tattoos.
And when
we run out of easy
silence,
we'll steal lines
from other people's
poems,
epigrams collected
from bathroom stalls.

We'll pay the band
to play
an extra hour,
hold each other
until we are weary,
or it starts to rain.

Kneel

*I am certain that the Lord, who notes the fall of a sparrow,
looks with compassion upon those who have been called upon
to part, even temporarily, from their precious children.*

—Thomas S. Monson

here at the threshold of war.
Wet your lips, smooth
the grime from your blistered feet.
No more walking,
this is home enough now, the moon
will be out soon
and ready to plug the bullet holes
in the sky with stars.
If it's worth praying, I will pray with you
in the language of olives.
We'll kneel on the grove floor, press
our lips to the chalky soil
and tend to love. Our breath will ink
the invisible names
of the dead onto the dampened leaves,
and when the sun
breaks the morning wide, the wind will dry
and carry them home. Follow.
There you will be greeted by mothers and wives,
and allowed to weep
against their breasts until your words smooth
into the tea kettle whistle.
Do not worry if the cups are cracked; they'll
still hold. Drink with honey and have
patience with the bitterness of grief.
It will try to tear
the thin-fleshed fruit, rush the feast.
Wait for it to rot
and open, for a single seed to fall.

When it does,
find your way here. Kneel, dig, pray.
Plant it deep in the blood-soaked earth.
Let your anguish be loud.
Even when the music of it cracks
every window for miles, stomp your feet bare
until exhaustion surrenders
to stillness. Roots will vine around your legs,
and then you will begin
to grow firmer in the flourish. Your branches
will grow strong enough
to hold sparrows.

MOJAVE

Christmas is out of place in the Mojave.
It's beautiful at night, when the pinkness turns
the mountain frame to background. We're driving it,

the route to L.A., and because there is only one,
when traffic stops, everything lacks options.

I think about the cactus leaves that have been tricked
by the unseasonable warm. How their bloom,
the color of rushed blood, glows in the low light,

so transparently that I want to touch your
face, shout *Happy Bloom Day,* but don't.

Instead, I draw upon the silver
needles of sagebrush that never show
seasons or age, what's to come in June

when rain rusts away the sheen. When I wake
next to you, childless, still. Or if we'll even
make it that far, stalled inside accidental spaces,

twilight soundlessly moving over our bodies,
an event so uninvited
that it feels like a celebration.

HEART SUTRA

I water the hydrangeas
to watch the water disappear.

ACKNOWLEDGMENTS

I would like to extend gratitude and recognition to the following editors and publications who first published versions of these poems:

"Alchemy", *Aperçus Quarterly,* June 2013

"Door County", *Blind Man's Rainbow,* Spring 2006

"He said", *Sceal, Premier Issue, Fall 2005*

"Filling Station God", Las Vegas Poets Prize Winner, May 2005

"Ivanpah Road", *Exit 13,* Spring 2006

"Kneel", *Mom Egg Review,* April 2015

"Mojave", *Red Rock Review,* Issue 18, Winter 2006

"Moths as Big as Hummingbirds", *Rio Grande Review,* Winter 2005

"Nothing, Arizona", *Desert Voices,* Issue 4 Volume 1

"One", *Comstock Review,* The 2008 Muriel Craft Bailey Memorial Award, Special Merit

"Scarring", *Aperçus Quarterly,* June 2013

"Tin Can Love", *Helen,* October 2014

"Traction", *Margie,* Volume Seven

"Ways to Worship", *Kalliope,* Spring 2007, Honorable Mention, Sue Elkind Poetry Contest

About the Author

Megan Merchant lives in the tall pines of Prescott, Arizona. She is the author of two chapbooks, *Translucent, sealed.* (Dancing Girl Press, 2015) and *In the Rooms of a Tiny House* (ELJ Publications, October 2016). Her second full-length collection, *The Dark's Humming,* was the 2015 Lyrebird Prize Winner (Glass Lyre Press, 2017). She is also the author of a forthcoming children's book through Philomel Books.

Glass Lyre Press

exceptional works to replenish the spirit

Glass Lyre Press is an independent literary publisher interested in technically accomplished, stylistically distinct, and original work. Glass Lyre seeks diverse writers that possess a dynamic aesthetic and an ability to emotionally and intellectually engage a wide audience of readers.

Glass Lyre's vision is to connect the world through language and art. We hope to expand the scope of poetry and short fiction for the general reader through exceptionally well-written books, which evoke emotion, provide insight, and resonate with the human spirit.

Poetry Collections
Poetry Chapbooks
Select Short & Flash Fiction
Anthologies

www.GlassLyrePress.com

CPSIA information can be obtained
at www.ICGtesting.com
Printed in the USA
FSOW02n2311120416
19129FS